T0129445

In Search of a Promise

Poems

Tundun Adeyemo

authorHOUSE®

AuthorHouse™ UK Ltd.
500 Avebury Boulevard
Central Milton Keynes, MK9 2BE
www.authorhouse.co.uk
Phone: 08001974150

First published by AuthorHouse 1/22/2009

ISBN: 978-1-4389-3489-1 (sc)

Printed in the United States of America
Bloomington, Indiana

This book is printed on acid-free paper.

A Little About Me

I have been writing since I was seven. It always fascinated me that I could record a piece of each day of my life. This book is the result of the chronicling of a season of my life.

Writing for me is therapeutic. Different things work for different people. I tend to draw strength primarily from the ordinary, everyday, common things I write.   Words have life. They have personality. Words when properly used, can heal. Its important that we learn to speak wholesome words as some words never die. I have chosen life, so I write and speak life.

These writings helped to find my faith. I hoped that as I wrote and poured my heart into writing, my faith would be restored. It worked!

I had lost my faith because it seemed all of a sudden, life was just hard. Life is hard. I have learnt that life can be difficult also. The key here is not to understand that no condition is permanent. Things will always get better. I actually lost sight of the big picture and my perspective of life was a bit wobbled. So, I suffered as well.

This book is the story of how a big Almighty God cared enough to use the very life I was bitter about, the little things in my life I had taken for granted to restore my faith. He built my faith through the same circumstances that tore it down. I had to come to realise that He does love me and nothing I have done, am doing, will do will change that fact. His love for me is eternal.

There is a lot to learn from Him. I am rediscovering myself and Him all over again. I am not at that place yet. I am taking it a day at a time. This is a life long experience for me, which started with the small little steps I took.

As you read these lines, its my hope that where ever you are, in faith or away from faith that you would fall in love with the Father again. Don't worry, He found me; he'll find you too! All errors are mine. No body to blame it on. So, I'll happily take it. I am counting on your forgiveness, and getting it better next time.

Tundun Adeyemo
March 2006

Acknowledgements

I didn't get up alone. God sent so many of people into my life at several times to bolster my faith. They did ordinary things in extra ordinary ways. Simply put, they held my hands as I considered my life! These people took me back to where I had lost the trail, and pointed me solely to Jesus.

I want to say to the many, many people who have been a blessing to me. I cannot mention you all: your reward is in heaven. May your rivers will never run dry.

I must mention some very special people. My mother and best friend: Mrs Aderemi Omolade Adeyemo. Our relationship is eternal. She made me see that as long as I have life, there is still hope. All I needed to do was to open my eye to see it. She gave me that courage to open my eyes.

My late father: Prince Aderemi Adeyemo. It's because of him I know I am destined for greatness. Such is the legacy he left me. I just know I will do great things. He believed implicitly and unquestionably in me. The memory of the righteous is blessed.

My pastors Agu and his late Ify Irukwu, Pastors Bioye and Biodun Segun and Pastor and Mrs Shola Adeaga. Some of these poems were written in church while I listened to Pastor Agu Irukwu. To put it simply, he inspires. I want to say thank you to Pastor Shola Adeaga who took time to listen to my questions as a father. He'll never know how much he validated me by taking time to answer my questions and showing me some misconceptions in my theology. He will never know how indebted I am to him for being there when I was hurting. This is a special Thank you.

Pastors Biodun and Bioye Segun just prayed for me. They knew I was in a situation, so they prayed. It was the best gift of all. Thank you for holding me down in prayers.

This is also for my Apple -;my 24 carat gold. We all have angels. I have concluded that you are mine. My other siblings; Toyin, Dupe, the latest addition to our family, my niece Princess Ounini-oluwa , Ayanfe- oluwaand to Adegoke Olanrewaju.

Some friends become family along the way: to Kofo, Babatunde and Banky. Kofo and I share most things in common. Our stories are the same, my struggle became hers and hers mine. One love.

Contents

Book 1

Book 2

Book 3

Book 1

Restored
Inspired by Psalm 23

This is what it comes down to
At the end of everyday
When I am tired and weary
Hands from above touch me
I am restored

When because of my frailty
I lose focus
When life brings too many
Distractions
And my heart is drifting to
A place no one really knows
Hands from above heal me
I am restored

Hands I cannot see
Hands that are always there
Hands that never complain
Hands as old as eternity

I don't always ask for restoration
I don't always cry for help
But as sure as the heaven and the earth
And day and night
I know I am restored daily

When the birds don't sing
And the seasons change.
All I need to do
Is wait for those hands
For surely, they will restore

I am restored through the night
My body is energized
The faith I lost
The dreams I gave up on
The time I squuundered
Is all restored

He is the restorer of my soul
He does all he needs to do
He mends, repairs, strengthens and heals
I am restored
My focus renewed
My strength rejuvenated
I start brand new
All because of His hands

My stained garments are washed
My heart is healed
My faith is restored
My body is stronger

I slept tired
I went to bed weary
A lot happened as I slept
An angel came and touched me
He wiped my tears and healed the scars
I am restored

I woke up brand new
I was different
I didn't even realize that the load
Was gone,
I didn't even know he had made me whole
For only He can restore
He is my Shepherd
He restores my soul
Every morning and night

I am not lost
Inspired by John 15

I am not lost
You are my Shepherd
I am not lonely
I am not hungry
You are always there

Your name is written
All over me
That's why I could not
Stay bound in sin
I could not stay in depression
I could not stay in shame
I could not stay in confusion
I am no longer in pain

You keep calling me
I hear your voice daily
You are my shepherd
I may stumble and fall
Along the way
It is sure I am getting back up

My hands in yours
Its really yours in mine
My frail hands cannot hold on to you
As tight as I want to
You are the one holding my hands
Through thick and thin
I can never fall

I don't have to fear I will loose your grip
I don't have to hold on so tight
Your grip is much stronger
I am rest assured that you
Are holding me
In your hands I am
The Father covers us both

I am not lost
I am not forgotten
I am- after all, the APPLE
Of your eyes
That's why they cannot touch me
They may try to hurt me
And they do try
At the end of the day
Because I am yours
They give up on me!

How can I be lost?
I know whose I am
I may be running in your party
I may be out with you
But, when my Daddy calls me
To Him alone I will go

I am not lost
Your love keeps calling me
You point me in one direction
The only way I know
Even if I was lost
Your sweet precious love has found me.

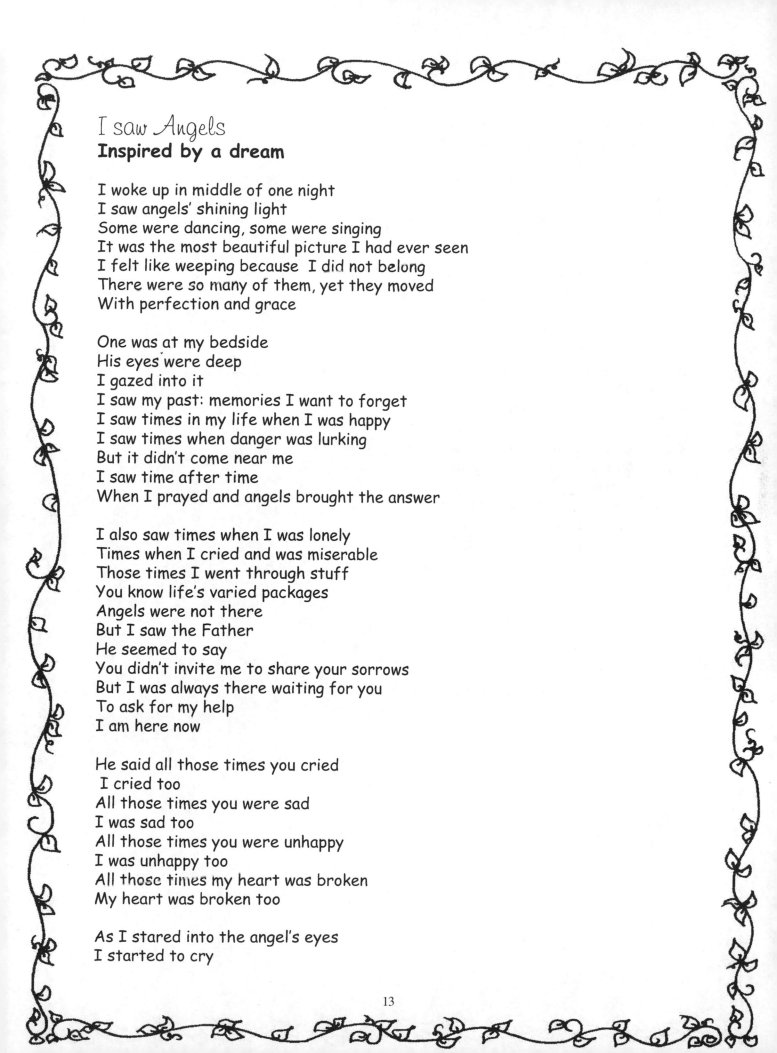

I saw Angels
Inspired by a dream

I woke up in middle of one night
I saw angels' shining light
Some were dancing, some were singing
It was the most beautiful picture I had ever seen
I felt like weeping because I did not belong
There were so many of them, yet they moved
With perfection and grace

One was at my bedside
His eyes were deep
I gazed into it
I saw my past: memories I want to forget
I saw times in my life when I was happy
I saw times when danger was lurking
But it didn't come near me
I saw time after time
When I prayed and angels brought the answer

I also saw times when I was lonely
Times when I cried and was miserable
Those times I went through stuff
You know life's varied packages
Angels were not there
But I saw the Father
He seemed to say
You didn't invite me to share your sorrows
But I was always there waiting for you
To ask for my help
I am here now

He said all those times you cried
 I cried too
All those times you were sad
I was sad too
All those times you were unhappy
I was unhappy too
All those times my heart was broken
My heart was broken too

As I stared into the angel's eyes
I started to cry

He asked me why
And I said I have been unhappy for a while
At that time, I thought
No one loved and cared for me
All those times I went to bed miserable
All those times I just suffered needless pain
For you were always there

He placed his hand on my shoulders
I stopped crying
He said these words that I will never forget
All is well. I am with you.
It was at that moment I knew
God has distinguished me
He has chosen and showed me love
For reasons I don't know.

I went back to bed, with his eyes watching me
I felt deeply peaceful and happy
I knew when I woke up
My life will never be the same again
It is a very beautiful feeling when
You have been chosen by God.

Cries!!!

This poem is a bit deep and sensitive. It was written at a very low time in my life. You must have felt like this before.

I am frustrated Lord!
I am tired of empty dreams
Just trying has gotten me here
Depressed, broke and exhausted
If you are really there
You will know that
I have come to the end of my self!
I am tired!

I reach out
My hands are too weak to stretch
I know you are there
But, I cannot reach you
I try my best
But it seems you have left my heart and life
There is really no life without you
That's probably why I feel
So empty right now
But how can you leave
When I am all yours?

Do not let ME wither Father
My pity party wont help me
Do not let me wither under this mayhem
Or under the stress
Or under my pessimism and negativity
Or under my shackles and shambles
Do not let me dry out
I fear my life is wasting away
My days have no meaning
I feel like Jonah as he sat under the tree
Or like Elijah when he ran away from Jezebel.

The world is pushing me
Life is pushing me
I am pushing my self
I can not articulate it
It hurts to relieve the memories
Sometimes I want to remain sad
At other times, I want to have a pity party.

My confidence is shaken
My life hurts so bad
I am not sure how to make it back up
I need to talk to someone
But my pain is stronger than words
Even the Father is probably weary with my words.

I begin to pray
But I feel my prayers bouncing off the ceiling
Please let hope yield in my heart
Let peace dwell with me
Let me recover my peace
Let me recover everything I have lost
I am tired of crying day and night
I am tired of not making a connection when I pray
I am tired of my weariness and constant desperation

Moments later......
I am now tired of my pity party
I am fed up with me, myself and I
I am done with my negativity
But, I dare to hope on you Father
For you are real
I am only here for a short time
You are forever and ever
I dare to hope that you can still this storm
I dare to believe that you can deliver me
I dare to believe that you can see my heart and
You can turn it all around for me

Whether or not you choose to sort me out
(He did sort me out, for I can now write that
He was there with me through it all).
It is in your hands
I believe you nevertheless.
I don't know how long my situation
Would last for
I don't know anything really anymore
What I do know is
I am now willing to look up

My Father talks

His response

I know

I know your life hurts
Notting can change the way you feel
I know the thoughts in your heart
I know what you are saying
And not saying
I know you in and out
I know how you got into your mess
I know how you will get out of it
I know how long more
I need you to know
 I am working all things out for your good.
You may find this cruel and unfair
But your pain and tears will work together
Your sadness will work together
I am going to give up on you
You will find your faith back

You cannot define yourself
By your own standards
Or by what you do, places you have been,
The things you have or what you have accomplished
Don't let anyone define you by these
Standards as well
You can only define yourself when you have me
Your problem is one of definition
Any definition away from me is flawed

You are hurting because you think
I have lost hold in your life
You think I enjoy you suffering
What you don't know is your life is in seasons
This season will pass
My will shall be done

Think about this
A woman touched the helm of my garment
And she became healed
I fed five thousand with only 5 loaves and 2 fishes
I am well able to replicate you

I can multiply all things
Only when you give them to me and leave them there
All I ask is that you believe in me
I can bring you out of this
In my own time
I can do all things for you
I will make your pain work for you
I know you have prayed
I know you trust me…. A little
A little faith is actually where to begin

Who are you listening to by the way?
The Lord or the world?
I change not, my words are eternal.
Are you not better of with me than
With any man whose words you cannot trust.

Dearest daughter
In your heart you need to understand
That I am your Father
I don't enjoy seeing you in pain
I delight in your happiness
Sometimes, I let my children go through
Stuff only because at the end they become better persons.
Look at you now! You have matured
And I am proud of you!

All I am asking is that you give me
Credit for being God
Trust me a little.
Its all I ask

Just honour me for who I am
For being the One who holds the breath in your nostrils
Who knows the real number of hairs on your head?
Who knew you before you were born
Who was there when you were a baby
Who has helped you all through out your life
Just honour me for what I have done
And what I will do
Is that too much for you?

The answers to your problems
Are all there within you
Your eyes are open, but

You cannot perceive
That in me is all
You'll ever need
Faith won't give up on you

This was not where you were last year
See how much I have blessed you
See how far you have come
Could you have done it all without me?
See all I have blessed you with
Have you noticed how good I have been to you lately?

All I ask·Dear Daughter
        Allow me to turn your seasons around
        Think about it!
        I have answered so many of your prayers
        My daughter I have not left you alone
        I am always with you
        I am holding you through
        Your darkest nights
        I saw you before you saw me
        I called you before you knew me
        I am after all
        The GOD of all the heavens
                What is there that I cannot do?

Night calls
a poem when God seems far away

I know you are there
Somewhere
It is just that I cannot see you
I know you love me terribly
But I cannot comprehend you
I know you care
But my heart cannot focus
I am a little confused right now
If you are with me
Why do I feel so empty?

Am I alone?
Can you hear me?
Can you see me?
So dear Jesus
As I go to bed
And you make house night calls
Please come by my bedside
And watch me through the night
I desperately need you

I am going to go to bed right now
Knowing you are here
I believe your Word
You are always with me
Send an angel at least to stand
Guard at the door!

What if I didn't love you?
My love for you

(Pastor Agu preached this message. It delivered me. I don't have the title or the date. I just know that as he preached, I started to write.)

On love
Human love is so fragile
It fluctuates with moods and circumstances
Human beings are fickle
They love you only when it is convenient
Human love can be so expensive
For humans being what they are
Will ask for something back
In return for their loving you
Human love is so seasonal and time measured
It simply vanishes when conditions are not right.

I see the way you love me
Sunday mornings in church
Especially all those little things
You whisper in my ears
Thinking I did not hear them
Sadly, you never mean the things
You say
You promise to love and obey me every day
We both know that's not what
You do.

I see the way you love me
When you cannot love or forgive
Believe me I know you love me!
Mornings you just go out without saying hello!
Days you spend without me
You love me all right!
You don't even introduce me to your friends
Or invite me into your close circles
You only come to me when you are in dire straits
You remember me when you are hurt
You only come when no one will have you
And you need love
You come only when you need to talk
But no one will listen

Human love
If I lived for your love
I would be heart broken now
Let me tell you how I love you
I looked at your shallowness
Your vanity, humanity, frailty, unbelief, doubt
Faithlessness
I remember the so many times
You take me for granted
Or changed your mind about me
I am not like you
I still do love you
I am love
Its who I am

You didn't ask me to love you
Before you were
I had paid the price for you
I had made it possible for you
To come to me
You didn't ask me to love you
I am love
My love keeps calling you

Everyday I give to you another
Opportunity to try to love me a little
For you struggle to love me
Most of the time

 I am the God many chances
When you cannot stand yourself
I love you
When you wont believe in yourself
I believe in you
When you let your self down
I never give up on you

I gave into your weakness
I came into the world
In a body like yours
I wanted to know what it felt like to be you
I died for you
Have you seen my scars?
See the nail prints on my hands and feet
I did it all for you

My death
What does it mean to you?

Every nail that was driven
Into my body was for you
Every hammer that pushed the nail in
Every pain I had to bear was for you
I remember carrying the cross-weary and tired
I was bleeding
I was weak
What led me on was you
I knew that one day you would
Need this sacrifice
I knew that one-day my death
Would mean the world to you

You needed me to die for you
I knew that my death would one day
I knew in my Cross was your deliverance
I knew the meaning of life
Starts and ends at Calvary
I knew that you cannot claim to love me
Without visiting the place where I died
I knew Calvary was going to be the place where
I could show you how much I loved you

History has it in its records
The earth cannot deny my death
I am not religion... I am the Lord
I am not an order - I am life
The world can testify that a man can
And he died and he resurrected
That man is Jesus
I am calling you.

I know one of your issues is that
You cannot get over your past
But, you have got to.
I have no interest in your past
I am interested in your future
And in your now

The truth is when I look at you
I see my son Jesus
Moreover, once you say you are sorry
Its all forgotten
The issue is
Can you forgive yourself?
I took care of your issues
When I died
All you need to do now
Is to look at me and live

My response to the other love ......

You cannot love me enough or love me
As I want to be loved
You cannot love me enough to soothe me
Your arms are only good for the night
When the hurts are less then
Its during the day I need your re-assurance
But you are simply never there
You cannot love me enough to take care away my deepest pains
I have come to realize you cannot really love me enough
It takes understanding to love
It takes time and commitment
To study a heart like mine
It takes dedication
To realize my unspoken words
You don't understand me
How then can you love me?
Well, you probably don't
Where were you last night?
Ha!!!
Whats worse, you don't even pick
Up when I call you
You don't love me!!!

This what I cannot stand
When I want to talk,
You turn on the TV or
Reach for the newspaper
When I just need for you call me
You say you are too immersed in work
To have remembered me
Half the time we talk
You seem only to want to talk about yourself!

I don't blame you though
Your love can only make
Sense
When I have found the father's love
You can never love me
Like my Father
Its only Jesus who can love me
Like I need to be loved

Jesus, your love is deeper
And accepting
You love me enough to
Understand my every up and down
You understand my deepest needs
Without making light of my pain
You know what I am saying when I sigh
Or when I cannot even articulate how I feel

You bear with me
Why did love have to die as a criminal?
Surely, you smile down at me for unreasonably
Thinking
That when I don't feel you
I am far away from you
But love is not a feeling.
How can that be, you love me?
My problem is that if you love me
Why am I going through such a hard time?
Why is my life so hard? Sometimes.

Jesus you are the true lover of my soul
In sickness and in health
In poverty and in riches
In destitution and in hopelessness
In peace and   instability
Jesus you are the true lover of my soul.
You understand me when I don't even understand
My self

I am complicated enough
I never seem to say what I mean
And lately,
I always seem to send the wrong messages!
Words don't seem to come out right
But you do understand my mess Father
And you still love me.

That's beautiful
I don't have to be anything else
You love me just the way I am
Jesus when you love me
You don't condemn me
Neither do you question me
Your love brings me hope

You are the one that can
Really only ever love me

I need love Lord
I need your kind of love
It is you I am looking for
Man cannot love me
As I want to be loved
I am looking for love
I probably wont find 'it'
Until I find you
And the pure love you
Offer every day to me
Beats the best love
I've ever had with any man

When your body bled, and you were
Bruised and gored
When the nails in your hands and feet
Couldn't hold you anymore
You remembered my name
You had compassion on me
You loved me till your very last breath
And you died
Just for me

Whilst you walked the earth
Reaching out to those whose pain only you know
You reached out to the hopeless
To those who had been broken by men, by life, circumstances
Those who had been broken by diseases
Who had been broken by relationships
The Bible records that you sat down
You took your time
And you healed them all
You touched every sensitive heart
Every broken heart
Every weary soul.
You sat in your majesty
And you healed
O my God!!!

In each and every page of this Bible
A promise of your compassion
Your faithfulness

I have just realized
That my needs are deeper
Beyond the scope of a man's touch
Wider than the capacity of any man
Its only you
That can find the balm to soothe
My aches, wants and needs.

Jesus says:
I want you to see that I am the only lover
Of your soul
I know your sorrows
Every man you have ever been with
Are counterfeits and liars
Every man who has ever told you 'I love you'
And failed were not able to love you like I can
I am the only one who can really love you
If you let me
I will love you every day
For all of eternity
I am eternity
I love you right
This very minute
I am love

I left my heavenly mansions
Endured the poverty of living
On a planet not as beautiful
As my heavens
I had to live 33 years without
The luxury of sitting on my throne
When elders bow down and worship me day in day out
Where angels in millions sing my praise for all eternity
Where I am the light
Where you can pick gold, diamonds
And all types of jewels on the roads
The houses are mansions carefully grafted
To reward each of my children
I am the King of my heavens
I had to give away all of that for you

Words are meagre and inadequate
To describe the depths of what your love is
Thank you for loving me
For my every day is an evidence of your love

If I really want to see it
You thought about me long enough
To give me the best you
Had to offer
You !!!!
You gave yourself to me
Incredible Father!
I am grateful you.
You came to die
Your everlasting love
Was written on the
Signs of the Cross
Your blood drained down
The wooden cross
Your broken body hung
In four different parts
Till you said 'it is finished'
Your redemption was done
How else would I know how you felt
Years later, you would direct me to the Cross
If I ever was in doubt.

I was that important to you
It still brings tears into my eyes
That you died for 'trash'
You would suffer so many things for a nobody
But because of what you have done
I am not trash
I am somebody
I am the head and not the tail

Even before I found myself
Even before I realized that
I am precious
I am diamond
You saw the gold in me
You still died

I was valuable enough
You could have changed
Your mind
You could have sent someone
Else to die in your stead
But you still chose to die
I don't know how many people

Would give their lives for me

My declaration...
I love you
I want to say thank you
For loving me
Long before I knew you
For giving yourself to me
Its too much of a gift
But it's a gift I accept
I have tasted several offers
Yours is still the best
I love you Father

You are
A God who is not content in loving me from afar
A Father who would stop at nothing to get my attention
A Father who delights in making me happy
A Father whose mercies are over whelming ...
It breaks my heart
A Father who gives second, third, fourth chances
No matter how far away I am
You are always calling me
Lord, your love humbles me right now
My eyes are moist, my heart is broken
Thank you for loving me
What amazing grace!!!
I don't deserve it, but I accept it
Thank you so much for loving me
And for
The promise that you will love me
For the rest of my life
                              Amen

The sun will always shine
For every girl whose heart has ever been broken

The sun had been shining all the while
The sun will always shine
Can man in his wisdom or
In the might of his technological prowess
Stop the sun from shining?
This simple truth obvious enough

The sun must shine daily in a golden sunrise
Urging all to draw from its strength
The miracle of a new beginning each day
At evening time
It sets with a song
Its colours work wonders
The wonders of its beauty seem to say
I shall not smite you by day
Nor by night

The sun was made to shine
It will remain even long
After our remains are buried
Its beautiful isn't it?
The sun will always shine

Its important to understand this
Simple truth
For as girls, most times we love with all
Our hearts
And in the process sometimes
Things don't go our way
Leaving us a little damaged and disillusioned.

What I have found out as a veteran of this process
Is that an ex- cannot stop the sun from shining
An ex cannot stop the Father from embracing you
Whilst the tears flow
An ex cannot stop the silent ministry of the Holy Spirit
Even when words cannot explain the pain
And the brokenness
The sun will always shine
If only, during these moments we have the
Courage to look up and dare to love again

Trust again, believe again, hope again
We must learn that for every day we choose
To die
The ex wins!
Life is more important than a man!
Any man!

Sunshine by sunshine
Sunset by sunset
The sun will always shine
The dark days are long over
My life can continue
Life has not had its last word
Faith once again has prevailed.

My depths had caused me to
Look to the heavens
To ask the God I have never seen
But in whom I strongly believe to help
Like all mortals
I needed help in many ways
I needed miracles
I needed to be healed
I needed justice
I needed him

Did He help?
At the time, it seemed
He had taken a long vacation
It seemed he had other important things on mind
It seemed he couldn't care less
Now, I know he was drawing me to him
I had to want something long enough
It was that thirst that brought me to him
In him were my answers

I wish I had the wisdom to write even finer words
These words are everyday, common, downright and plain old true
God can never fail.
There will be times when it looks like you are falling
It only seems like it though
You will never fall down
Well, even if you do
Like all saints who have gone before
You will make a come back

You will rise again
You will laugh again
You will believe again

 What you are doing with my life
I can never tell
There was a time in my life
I thought a man brought the sun
He was a very sweet man though
He made me laugh
I equated him with the sun
After a while, he left.
He took ·away with my sun
Or so it seemed.
Even though the sun was shining
It was very dark in my heart
The truth was that the sun
Never stopped shinning
He walked out with my sun
But the sun stood still
Observing and recording my pain
I thought I would just die!
I didnt have the heart to face another day
That was then
This is NOW

I suppose without any impediments
I want to stand
As tall as I can be with the sun in my focus
To serve the God who made the sun
And brought me out of the darkness

My body is tired at the moment
Its late I guess
But my spirit is alive
Like it has never been
I have discovered
The deepest truth of all

I will never die
Let me explain
From sunrise to sunset
God remains the same
I will age gradually
27-37-47-67-87-107

And one day
I will die
Expectedly, but suddenly
But my spirit will never die

I will live in heaven with my Saviour
Who hung a tree because he knew
I needed him there so he could bring me into
A place where He rewards
A place where there are no tears
A place where my happiness would be forever
The sun will always shine
I will make the best of all my days under the Sun.

I am returned to Jerusalem with mercies
Zechariah 1:16

Where ever you are right now
At peace or at war
Broken or whole
Sad or happy
Single or married
Young or old
Man or woman
Rich or poor
Strong or weak
Hungry or full
Fat or thin
It doesn't matter

What ever you are doing right now
Where ever you are right now
I am returning to you with mercies
I am listening to all your prayers
I am delivering you from every
Thing that has held you back
I am giving you strength to dare
To dream again
Laugh again
Hope again
Love again
Try again
Build again
Write again

I am giving you the grace
To live again
You don't have to give up
You don't have to give in
You don't have to be afraid
You don't have to let each
Day pass you by
You can be all you want to be
I have given you a dream
Different from all others
Different from most
Because you are unique

You are not just an ordinary person
You are spectacular
You are a shooting star
You are an angel
You are priceless
You are a diamond
You are special
You are my Apple and my babe

I hear you whenever you call
It may take time
It may be a while
But believe it I do
Not forget prayers
I have your tears in a bottle
I am always on time
I love you too much
I have decided to grant your heart desires
I have decided to wipe your tears

I have decided to listen to your unheard prayers
I have seen your affliction
I am visiting your pains
I know your sorrows
I am here with my mercies
And my grace
To meet every need of your life
For I am returned to Jerusalem with mercies.

Prophecy
say Amen

The clouds around you are heavy
And I am about to fall rain on you
Heavy rain not to wash you away
But in measures to fill every corner
Of your life

I am about to rain upon you
Answers to your prayers
My rain of deliverance
Of healing
Of grace
Of peace
Of wisdom and justice
A rain of my visitation
Are you soaked yet?
For its now raining ….
My rain of peace
My rain of beauty
My rain of gold and diamond
My rain of healing and comfort
My rain of milk and honey
My rain of manna
My rain of more than you can
Ever ask or think

You are now blessed
Walk into the sunshine of my abundance.

Book 2

The birth of hope

Questions
Deeper reflections

I am well aware of my humanity
And my frailty
I do not have answers
To all my questions
I need constant light
To know how I am going to get
To where I am going
Right now in some ways
I know I have gotten to the end of this road
Even though the journey is not over

In my deepest parts, I must admit
I need help greater than me
I need hope from only you
I ask so many questions
The mathematics don't add up
So many unexplained puzzles
So many 'but whys?'
So many things to worry about
Who knows the end?
Who can answer the whys?
Who can tell me why
Some babies are still born?
Or where little babies go to when they die
Who can tell me how
Are animals in heaven?
Are their wasps, butterflies, millipedes and snakes in heaven?
When animals die, do they go to heaven?
Or are they perished for ever?

Who can tell me how wounds heal?
How time is calculated?
Who holds the earth?
What happens when we sleep?
Are angels real?
Who can explain the principle
In reaping a thousand when you
Sow only ten?
Who can tell the language babies speak
Or who can decipher when the birds are hungry?
Who can tell the end?

Can you walk on water?
Why does the spirit realm control
The physical
Who has ever seen angels?
Or walked in the valley of the shadow of death to
Tell the tale?
Who can confirm that demons are real?
Or that death is a person
I really don't want to know that!
Who can explain the mysteries of salvation, of baptism, of faith and trust?
Who can touch the invisible or hold the untouchable

On this side of eternity
Are there answers?
You don't need answers to all your questions
I am the answer, God seems to say
Questions are for philosophers and scientists
It gives them work to do!
Yours is only to believe
Some things are too much for you to understand
Some things are too difficult to be explained
All you need is me
This is what you really need to know
I am more than enough for you
I am going to be with you
All the way

All answers are in you
To find the truth
You need to calm down
You will need to be at peace
In your self
Then you will find your answers
You don't need a prophet, a pastor, a bishop
Your answers are there within you

Thank you Father
For these are eternal words
Words that will see me through this life
And to the one beyond
I shall not fear whatever life brings

I will not fear
Not fear for rejection or loneliness
I am with you

You were with Abraham
And he died a good old age
You were with Daniel in the lion's den
With Sarah when she delivered
With Abel when Cain slew him
With Noah as he built the ark
With Moses while he parted the Red Sea
With John the Baptist
With Joshua conquering cities,
With Joseph as he was thrown in the pit and as he was in prison
With Jesus on the Cross
God Almighty
I will not fear
You are with me in all I do

I am the God of Abraham
Fear not, I am with you
I will bless you
Will you please open my eyes?
To the potential of what I can do
When I understand that you are with me

Lord I turn to you
You have asked me not to fear
You never failed Abraham and his wife Sarah
In the hope of your promise to them
It is said of Abraham
That he staggered not at the promise
He held on inspite of the contradictions
Of his situations
He held on against all hope
Hope against all hope
He held on even when
It was just silly
To hold on
He held on when others laughed at him
He held on even when he was lonely and in need
He just held on
He knew something we know but always forget
Faith always wins

As I go through my many days
Give me the kind of hope Abraham
Had which was solely in you
May I never fear life

And whatever all it brings
May I truly see that with you on my side
There is notting we cannot conquer
For you are with me
And whats even better,
You will bless me

Dear Tundun
Do not be afraid
I am always with you
It may not seem like that
Remember that Peter did not drown
While he walked on water
He started to sink only because he kept his eyes off me
You are sinking because your eyes are not on me
You are lost in your storm
You cannot figure it out all by your self
And you have taken the right from me to help you
If peter did not drown, why should you?

Did I forget Jesus on the Cross?
Or was He lost in hell?
You think I have forgotten you
You have a situation in your life for a reason
And you are coming out

You blame me for one major loss in your life
You have blown this so out of proportion
Give me credit for that which I do
Give me credit child!!!
I am the Lord.

I say it again
Do not panic
Do not be afraid
I will give you strength
When you need it
You have given up on me
It is so sad
You have lost your faith
But how can you when I change not?

Do not be afraid
I am here to help you
Notting is too difficult for me to do

I will bring you out of all things
In a matter of time
Your life is a challenge
This season will pass
This moment will come and go
And come again

You have to make up your mind
To seek my help daily
All the way
You have to learn to believe
In the things you cannot see
You have to learn to find me
In the very little things
That's where I am
In places you do not expect to find me
Even in your heart

If only you saw your end
You will know that just like everything else
Your troubles have a time scale
Its almost morning now
I am the Lord
I hold it all in my hands
The mornings, the nights,
Your days.
I know the day your end
I know when to visit you
I am always on time even
When it seems late to you
I am the Lord

Dear child
            Will you believe me?

I am the One who feeds the birds of the air
I clothe the lilies of the valleys
I am the Ancient of Days
The wisdom of the Ages
The never changing God
Even when you deny me
There is no one like me
In the heavens and beneath the earth
I cannot deny myself
I am the double-breasted God

I give good gifts to my children
I am faithful to you
I am the truth
I can never lie to you
All my promises to you are true
You can take my word on it

I am
I was
I am for all eternity
I am THE ROCK OF AGES
Are you going to let me be your Rock?
I am your healer. Will you let me heal you?
I am your father
Can I father you?

Trust that I am holding your hands through life
I have got you covered
You have to believe me
Can I lie to you?
Have I ever lied to you?
The fire will not burn you
This experience will only make you better.

The blessing
The Bible

Therefore I give you the dew of heaven
And the fatness of the earth
And plenty of corn and wine
Let people serve you
And the nations bow down to thee
Be lord over thy brethren
And let thy mother's sons bow down to thee
Cursed is every one that curseth thee
Blessed be everyone that blessed thee

AMEN

A Prayer Right Now

Dear Jesus

I cannot really connect to heaven right now
I have lost my faith
I have lost my belief that things will get better
I feel stuck
I am tired of running
Tired of always worrying

Right now, I am just tired
I want to go back to bed
Crawl underneath my duvet
And wish all my problems away

Will you start by giving me new hope?
For my hope is dead and buried perhaps
I don't believe anymore
I have had too many disappointments
I am feeling really fragile right now
Will you re-kindle my hope in you?
Will you give me a reason to live again?

I need to know you
For myself
My answers might just be in you.
May your arms lead me to find you
I ask for healing
I am hurting
I ask for restoration
I ask for peace within
I ask for that quiet confidence
In your everlasting arms.

Ask
this is the message of the gospel

I don't know how
But, I ask that my life might inspire anyone
Who is   honest enough to admit
That they get weary sometimes
That they are discouraged and just tired
I ask that you would be near all those
Who need to hear from you
All those who need to know
That you are the God who is able
See one through whatever life throws at them.

I ask that as I sleep tonight
I might see heaven's beauty
I might hear music from angels
And the heavenly choir
I ask that I may wake up
Feeling the depths of your love for me
I have felt it before
Please can I feel it again?

I pray that the morning would come with
Confidence in the One under whose eyes we slept
I pray that we find the promised hope
Of a better future in tomorrow

Finally Father
You did say
Ask for anything
I ask for my passion back
I need a zest for life
I need grace to find You
Everyday and for
All of my days
Amen

Almighty God
the softer I talk the calmer I feel

Please change my lingo forever
For in my speech there is life and death
Give me a vision of my tomorrow
That I may dwell in the hope that my life
Has some meaning
.... And that meaning is in you.

If I could just see that there
Is a tomorrow-in today
Then maybe
I would take time
To savour the delicacies of today

I am at a quarter of my life already
I need hope
I need hope to smell the roses
Hope to believe in every sunrise
Hope to give it all back to you at sunset
Hope to dream again
Hope to believe that the best is yet to come
Hope to love again

I ask that you change my words forever
Help me speak of the hope you have given to me
To those whose lives have lost its meaning
To those whose circumstances
Have squeezed life out of them
To those whose pain they can hardly bear

Let me be music to someone who needs to hear some
Let me be poetry to someone
Who needs these words
Let me be healing to someone
Whose life is hurting
Let me be a song
Someone can play.
Amen

Bethel
inspired by my own walk with God

I am
The Covenant keeping God
I am bringing it all together
For you
That's who I am
The God of your tomorrow
The God who never forgets a promise
Nor a vow

Do you know how many of your prayers
I have answered?
I bet you have lost count
Do you know how good I have been to you
Lately?
I am the God who never sleeps
I am the One who keeps every promise

The God of covenants
The God of all life
I am the God of Bethel
I am in the secret place of your tears
I am in the inner sanctuaries of your heart
I am where no one has been
Where no man has the right to invade
I hold it all together
I am the One who keeps you going
I am the One who prospers you
I am the One who remembers you
I am the One who seeks for you
I am in your silence
I am in your vows

I see your fastings and denials
I have your tears in my bottles
I see your offerings and your good works
Do you think I can forget you?
A mother can forget her children
But can I forget you?
Can I forget the day you decided to follow me?
Can I forget your pain?
The way you laugh

And sing
Can I forget you?

I am the God of Bethel
I can never break any promise I make to you
Let all men be liars and I alone be true
I cannot break my word to you
My covenant with you is
'It shall be well with you'.
It is well with you
I am the God in Bethel
Beyond your Bethel
I am still God.

Pleasant surprises

Happy moments

Thank you for surprises
For meeting every need
I know you don't really expect me to say this
But thank you for helping me out this month
That was a miracle!

You are beautiful in every situation
I see your hand in everything
Then it makes sense
Moses, your friend described you as
Merciful, faithful, forgiving, abundant
In goodness and in truth
John, whom you loved, said it is because
Of your love that we have the power to become
Power to become **all** we can be in you

I just want to say thank you for every breath
For my body organs
For being able to do the little things
Like to wash my own back
Smile
Eat a potato omelette and much more!
Get up from bed
Communicate my feelings
Sit without assistance
For number 1 and 2
For a good night rest
Every night

Thank you for my sanity
Thank you for health to work
Thank you for every thing
I don't want to be an ingrate
These are two words I don't say enough
Two words you don't hear enough
Thank you
.... Especially for loving me the way you do
I am simply over whelmed dear Jesus
I made it through another month!

Changes
for my Lord

I am the Lord, I change not
To what do I change?
For whom do I change?
I mean what I say and I
Say what I mean if
I did not mean it
I wont say it

You change
You grow old
At one time you are devout
The other, you hate devotion
At one time you love me
The next, you cannot find an hour for me
At one time you make vows
The next, you break all these vows

I change not
I am
I never change
I never grow old
I know the end of all things
All you know is this minute
The next minute is mine forever to know

I am the Lord
I change not
When I say I love you
I mean it
Even when you go against me
When you fight me
When you wont spend time with me
I still love you
I am love
Patient and kind
The God of many chances
I cannot change
I am who I am
For all eternity
I am.

I am that I am
Exodus 3:14

I am so conscious of my mortality
I know one day it breathe my last breath
I am 27 this year
I have spent almost a quarter of my life already

Father,
You are the ever-present one in time
Trouble and great happiness
You are in the past
Right now
And in the future

As I go through my life and
My constant battles with excesses
I must be a size zero!!!
Let me remember
The I AM
When I worry about my bills and income
When I make plans and there is no
Money to pay for the plans
Let me remember that you are the I AM

When I sign by reason of issues
Or the hardness of my life
 Let me remember you are the I am
You are everything I need in every situation
You are my strength, comforter, wisdom
You are the I am
 You are my ever present help in times of trouble.

For you were when I was broken in
Unpleasant relationships
When men rejected me
When I struggled with my identity and self worth
When I was rejected
When I was lonely and wounded
When I sought and no one was there to find me
When my phone did not ring
When I cried and dried my own eyes
When I hurt and could not share my pain
You were

Help me remember that
You are the I am
And that you are always there for me
To help me when I am in distress
Help me remember that
All I ever need is in you.

Music to you
thinking about Psalm 150

Holy Spirit
Make my life sweet and beautiful
Let me be the song you sing daily.
Every morning I want to wake up
With you
I want to understand that
Its only your grace that has kept me
Through the night

I want to be your heartbeat
I want to be your Apple
Tender and beloved
I invite you into that very special
Place of my heart
Where you are Lord
I love you
You are the lover of my soul
You are all mine
I want to love you much more than
The poet and psalmist David did
I want my life to be song to you.

If you have to
I know you have already started to
Process me Lord
Rid me of every thing that is not of you
Till I become music to you

You looked at David and you laughed
He provoked you in so many ways
He knew how to get you to dance
He was a very beautiful and special song to you
You looked at Jesus
He was MUSIC
Jesus was your heartbeat
He was you.

That is what I want to be
More than a song
More than a beat, more than a dance
I want to be music

I want my spirit to be sweet before you
I want my life to bring rapturous melody
I want to be an orchestra
In your eyes, to your ears, to your heart.
Every day I live

I can only be that
If I deny my self daily
Pick up my cross and follow you
Yeah!!!!!!
Its hard you know...
But not impossible
I will try everyday Lord
To die to self
To be more like you
Then and only then
Will I become music to be played before you.

Amen

This is who I am
For Apple

I enjoy writing.
I have kept a journal for years
I believe strongly that every day is special
I believe I must number my days for I wont always be here
I have known this since I was 7
I started by writing about things which hurt me
I tried to record those memories I wanted to keep
For a lifetime
I have not changed much since then
 I have stopped writing about boys only

Now it seems I write more about
The Man in my life
My friend, husband, daddy, father, saviour, redeemer
This book is all about him
I write also hopefully to bring
Healing to hearts
We all need to understand and accept
That life cannot be a bed of roses
All the time
There would sometimes be grief, sadness, pain, loneliness, heartaches, and discontentment
But this is not where it all ends
There will always be another story.

Nothing in life is permanent
Life is never a straight path
Things are not all that easy
The grass is not greener on the other side
If we can see the clear picture
The picture of our eternity and mortality
Then it all makes sense.
Our lives, our missions
The words we speak, the way we live
All makes sense

This is who I am
A writer
A dreamer
I am just hoping He would use that
 which HE HAS GIVEN ME

The ability to put my feelings into words
I hope these words touch the heart of somebody
I hope it makes a difference
I know it has
It will
If you will
This is my own legacy.

This is who I am
I must write to bring
Sweet praises to Him
Who loves me better than I can love myself
Who understands me more than anybody I know
I want to make him proud of me

Its not likely I would start a revolution
Or conquer cities or do mighty great things
Like that
It not likely I would make scientific discoveries
That would change the course of mankind
And I might
Can you tell?
Its not likely I would fight with tigers and beasts
Like the Romans did at Ephesus
A lot is not likely but not also not impossible
What is likely is that I will keep writing

Life is a gift
I am giving it back to you.
The many days I have lived already
And the ones I am yet to see
I give it all back to you
In these days and in the ones ahead
Let me find you as treasure
And incomprehensible beauty
To last for all my days.

                              Amen

Survivor
For me

I believe you can find hope in words
Hope to carry on regardless
Of where you are right now
Regardless of where you have been
Regardless of what has happened to you
May you find
Hope for that spring in your steps
Light in your darkness
Whatever that may be
Hope to embrace
Hope to heal
Hope to dare
Hope to persevere
Hope to go on

If noting else
You have come this far
Still the same, still breathing
A toast then to you
A celebration to your now
A glass of cheers raised in your honour
You have over come many mountains
Imaginary or otherwise
You have scaled a mighty ocean
You have fought with bears and lions
You are still here
You are a survivor
You are a champion
Some could not get where you are
Some died on the way
Some went insane
Some are in hospital
But you are here

A toast to you
Simply for being you
For hanging in there
This poem is for you
You are a survivor just like me
You have been to hell and back
Your eyes are focussed on heaven
You cannot fail
He means more to you now than he ever did.

..........That was why you had to go through all you went through.
To find Him.

Night time
For Princess Ini

Its night time
I would like to check with you
That my feelings are still the same
They haven't changed
I still love you
I made a couple of mistakes during the day
But my allegiance
Is still there
I am still for you
All the way

Could you please not mind my anxiety,
Distractions
Frustrations
Moments when my sights are off you?
When I have gotten momentarily off key
I have a lot more to write
But I feel at the moment I am just drifting away
Saying well
Notting really important

If nothing else
Would you record eternally that right now that
I love you
Tundun
　　　　blowing sweet kisses to heaven.

Je t'aime

I love to spend every day of my life
My mornings and nights
In quiet and passionate recognition of who You are
In search of all you are and all you promise to be
I want to adore you
Would you show me how to love you?

I want to wake up every morning
Singing the songs you give me
This poem is about saying thank you for your
Mercies which are new every day

This is my way of saying you are the best
My way of saying you are loving when I am not
You remember me when I forget
You have shown me mercy time and time again
I want to say thank you
For your love
Thank you the peace you give me
Holding me every day
Speaking with quiet words of strength to me
Watching over me as I sleep
For being closer than my brother
These words just don't seem right
They seem really hollow on light of all you have done for me
Inadequate in light of all
I have received from you
Thank you

Will you please show me how to daily praise you
How to walk with you?
To call you one by one by the names you bear
To call you
The Lord my beautifier
For you are beautifying my life

The Lord of Mercy
For you have shown me mercies
The Lord of hope
You have put hope and gladness in my heart
The Lord my sanctifier
You have made me whole

The Lord my strength
I had experienced your strength many times
My refuge
My song: my sweet song
My new song
My hope
You give me daily hope
A reason for living
My heart leaps.
I want to know only you
To be satisfied with all of you

The God I know

You come in different ways
As the lily of the valley
The ray of hope in life's deepest valleys
He gives beauty for ashes
He is the rivers of life
When you need answers and hope
There is no end to the abundant life
He brings
With Him life gets better and better
He has a way of making all things new

He is Mighty
For those looking for strength
He is the Rock, Fortress, and strength of Judah
For those scared, He is the Lion of Judah

You are more than everything
To the merciful, you are merciful
To the kind you are kind
You are every thing I want you to be
I have known you as my beautiful for my situation
Hope in darkness
Hope in bereavement
Hope in distress
Hope in loss
Hope in brokenness
Hope in misery

You are the hand that has guided
Me all my life
Healed me time and time again
He is my healer
I ask you that your will to be done

Your hand guides in life and in death
In life through the storms
Through situations
Through stuff
I cannot discuss
Through pain that tears cannot contain
Through the insecurities of our present life
I tend to over emphasize the fact that my problems

Are big
But, you are bigger.
Bigger than the biggest mountains
Stronger than the strongest winds

The God I know
When judgement calls, mercy cries out
When I almost perish, he rescues
When he has had enough of me,
He kicks into longsuffering
He will stop at notting to get to me
He wont leave you in the dumps
He wont walk out on you
He wont give up on you
He never gets tired of me

Do you sometimes wonder?
Written years ago

Some times I wonder will I live to be 40, 50 or 70?
Will I live to see my grand children?
Will I ever be happy?
Will I ever do all I want to do?
Will I ever be all that I want to be?
Will I ever see my Apple again?
Will I ever be united with my father; Aderemi Adeyemo?
Will I ever travel the world? -America, Bermuda, Australia, Canada, China,
France?
Will I ever get married?
Will I ever find true love?
Will I ever have a child?
Will I ever be called mummy?

I am 26 this year
My heart is young I want to fly
I still want to soar
I still have dreams
My body is not old.
My breasts are still firm
My tummy may not be flat
As I have gained some weight
But, I am still young
My face radiates my youth
My skin is still so smooth
Will I one day see these same breasts lay flat
These same skin, rough and weary
This same body tired?
Will I ?

I suppose I will
Life still smells the roses
Enjoying the summer heat
The sun came up this morning but I missed the awesome sunrise
My armpit hair is grown back, but I missed the early sprouts

What is life?
Sharing a secret joke with your self, enjoying a quiet dinner, listening to a
tape
I love life
I might not have seen too much of it, but I love life

I want to live and not die
Life is in my every waking moment.
In my every breath
In every thing I do and see
This is my life,
This is where I am right now
Just taking a moment to look at how far I have come to get right here.
Before I begin my next lapse.

Daddy
This is for daddy Remi

Time has healed me surely
Time has stopped the tears
Time has made it better
But time cannot take you away from me

Time cannot erase the memories
Time cannot take away your legacy
I won't let time ever take
You away from me

Some say because you are with Jesus
Its not healthy to remember you
I don't care what they think
You will always be my daddy
Notting is ever going to change that!

I have a lot of memories
 I am holding on to
I still have pictures
I still remember your words
Did I just say time has stopped the tears?
I lied
I am crying right now

Your legacy leaves on
I don't hurt like I used to
Its not as painful
But its still so wrong that
You are not here

I don't think its fair
That you missed my graduation
My marriage, your grandchildren, this book
You missed most of my life
I know you are watching from heaven
But its not the same
Sometime I wonder if you were here
Whether my choices would have been different

We did say goodbye

I am thankful for the opportunity
I never had the chance to celebrate you
You had an accomplished life though
How can I tell the world
That you were the best dad in the whole wide world?
How can I tell the world
Its because of you I know
I am destined for heights

You believed absolutely and unquestionably in me
You showed me the pleasure in books
You taught me the mystery of religion and the church
Its because of you I know I will make it
I just know I will be great
I will do great things

I know you are watching
Over me
Over us all (mum and my siblings)
We shall meet again
For now, its only Adieu.

Book 3

All the poems here are dedicated to my mum and best friend.

You are love

You probably don't think I mean these words
It doesn't matter
But I do love you
You have seen me clean and dirty
Holy and defiled
Sad and happy
Right and wrong
Winning and losing
Yet you still love me

I love you
This is all I want to say
I have been difficult with you
I have not given you any credit
I take you for granted
Yet I am because you are
I love you
Thank you for loving better than I can love myself

The Love of a Father

It can get better than this
Life was meant to go on and on
So one day, we can look back
And tell our children the tale
Of your faithfulness
We can tell our children how
Much you mean to us

In my imperfections
I ask for your perfection
In my ugliness, your beauty
In my doubt, faith
In my weariness, strength
In my loneliness, your friendship
In my sickness, your healing
In my solitude, your peace
In my ignorance, your wisdom
In my chores, your peace

I have asked for this before
I ask for you
And the beauty of your kingdom
In my heart
For all eternity.

I've got you

Let me know that you love me
Even when I wake up first thing in the morning
Let me never start a day without feeling
The sweetness of your love
Let me never doubt the reality of your love for me
Nor the reasons why you love me

If the truth were to be told
I know I am a diamond
No one can be me like me
But I struggle with feelings of inadequacies
I always need to know that I am loved
That I am loved by you
That you are all mine
And I am all yours
I need to know that I am special to you
I do not have to do anything to get your attention
You love me just the way I am

I have got you
When I think there is no one to understand
To hear me
To listen to me
To pray for me
I have got you
I don't know why you are so kind
And why you are so merciful to me
I really don't need to know why
I only ask to be loved unconditionally
Please don't stop loving me
Help me to reflect on the fact that when I have you
I have it all

I ask for you

You are the sum total of all I need
You are beauty when I feel ugly
You are my peace in storms
In confusion, my teacher
In pain, my healer
In need, my provider
In suffering, my healer
In life, my hold
In life, my friend
In death my Saviour
You are everything I need in every situation I get into

For the rest of my life
I ask for you
Every day
A bit of you
Till I can fully comprehend the depths of living
Under your loving wings
I ask for You.
For all that you are in my life
I need you so much
I cannot do anything without you
I have learnt that
Any life without you is meaningless and useless
I ask for you
To have and to hold
I ask for you
For all of you
From now, every day, till the day I die.

Mummy mii

The Lord has blessed me in so many ways
Being my mother is God's special way of
Loving me
I want to celebrate you
I know these words are inadequate
To describe how much you mean to me
I will try

I don't have too many friends
You are the One person I can open up to
When I hurt, I don't have to hide
I can come clean
I feel as though there is notting I cannot say to you
I have never felt judged or criticized
 Only understood
I am that age where sometimes I only need
To have a good conversation
We may be miles apart
But somehow you know when I need to talk
And you call
There have been so many times when as I begin
To call, your text comes through

You have supported me through many trials
I want to acknowledge every gift with thanks
 You always remember to call
Its always sweet when you say
'I only wanted to hear your voice'
You have given me the strength to begin new chapters
And to close old doors
You have helped me see life from fresh perspectives
Each time I wanted to give up on life
You have taught me to love singing as you have a heart for songs
There are songs we share that I am going to pass on to my own
Children
You have blessed me by loving me
You have been there when I just needed company
Sometimes you don't say much, you only listen
When away from God or in doubt of his goodness
I look into your life and I remember God's faithfulness
You are my constant Christian witness

I am blessed to have you
Thank you for being there for me
For your support, faith and confidence
For your unflinching loyalty
For your many prayers
For constantly hoping and watching out for me
For rent money and all monies when broke
For loving me moments unconditionally these many years
Thank for being my number 1 fan
I love you so much
You are the greatest mum in the world

A new beginning

This is what you offer to those
Who are washed by your blood
To those who have accepted that one
Price you paid for all time
This is what you give to all
Who have ever said
Who are saying
And who will say
I surrender it all
I have you engraved in the palm of my hands
Each time I open my hands
I see you
Your Blood cleanses and washes
The Blood will never be shed again
Its been shed once and for all
This is the new beginning for all
Those who would dare look up
From what ever and where ever

Your heart shall live

You heart shall never die
If you know me
If you know my thoughts for you
If you wake up with me
Go to bed with me
Spend your days with me
Let me into your heart
And let me love you like
Only I can

Let me be all no one has ever been to you
Let me heal and restore you
You will never die is my promise to you if
You believe my Word
 my promises
 my passion
You can know me my child
I am never far from you.

Can I ask you then to
Take a walk with me
Into the impossible?
My ways are life and peace
Your heart shall live
If you seek me

Ask

I did say to you 'ask and you shall receive'
You do well, when you ask
You ask for cars and houses
You ask me to bless you
And I have
You are enjoying peace like you never have before
I have perfumed your life
I have removed the pain and the dirt
I have filled your life
With the sweet aroma of my presence
Your life is very beautiful

I told you to ask
But, you never ask for ME
You never ask to see me
To know my heart
To touch my garment
To understand my passion
To love me
With all of my heart, soul and mind
To discover me
You ask for the world
But never for me
Am I not more than the world to you?

I am love
I am more than enough for you.
I am the wisdom of the ages
I am everything you need me to be
I am the I am
All you ever need is in me
You are because I am
Go on Ask for me

Where did I get it wrong?

Where did I go wrong?
What are my wrongs
You have ignored me
You have acted like you have made it on your own.
What did I do make you turn your back on me?
Please tell me what my offences are
I need to know
All I have ever wanted was the best for you
My thoughts for you are perfect
For your peace and success
It was me: there for you
When you were broken hearted
I was there for you
when you failed
And you struggled with depression and disappointments
It was me when you were broke and busted
I, when your body ached
It was me who stilled the storms
Me who healed your wound
I have been there every second of the way
I have shared your glories and triumphs
Your grief was mine
Your sadness was mine
Your pain was mine
Your tears were mine
I have been at every walk with you
I have been your Father
You hid in me when you needed restoration as you healed
I am the only one who has never disappointed you
I am the only faithful friend you have
Yet you ignore me
You know that hurts me
I want to spend time with you
I want to be with you
I love you dear child
Where have I gone wrong?

I got my faith back

I know its taken all year
But I have found you back
You were never lost
I just refused to see your side of things
I was happy in tears
I wailed till I was sick and tired
Now, I have found your loving kindness
If only I trusted you all that time
The pain I went through was not necessary
Time has been wasted away from you Lord
I am home now
This is where my heart is
Home is to know and understand you
Home is where all faith begins and ends
My journey begins here
I Love you Father
                    - Good night

Epilogue

I hope you have enjoyed reading this as I have writing it. I got my faith back. You have followed my thoughts, my struggles, my life basically. I have healed, I have learnt and still learning that I walk my faith and not by sight. My Father is holding my hands, I don't have to be afraid of stepping into my tomorrow.

You may need a new beginning. You may just need the Father. Why not start it with Jesus today? Its simple. Simply confess all your sins and ask him to be your Lord and Saviour and that's it really. If you need more information about this person that has changed my life. Write to me by email. My email is Tundun. Adeyemo@gmail.com.

I look forward to hearing from you.